Quiet Images

*Photographs and Text
by
Jane M. Rohrbach*

*Closing verse printed
with permission from
UUA Publications.*

Published by Jane M. Rohrbach
P.O. Box 3
Robesonia, PA 19551
windowsjmr@aol.com

Printed and bound by
LithoTech, Inc.
Reading, Pennsylvania

Copyright © 2002
by Jane M. Rohrbach
ALL RIGHTS RESERVED

ISBN: 0-9725241-0-X

INTRODUCTION

When I was twelve years old, my father gave me my first 35MM camera. I was going to accompany my parents on a business trip to Europe and would miss the first few weeks of eighth grade, so my assignment from the school superintendent was to document our trip and prepare a travelogue for the Rotary Club. Needless to say, the assignment was great fun for me and I have been enjoying travel and photography ever since.

Over the years, nature photography became my primary focus and in 1995 I attended my first photography workshop with Rod and Marlene Planck in Michigan. During that first workshop in the field, I managed to fall into a bog and do many other silly things. In spite of all that, I was invited to future workshops and continued on to improve my photographic skills and develop close friendships with people who share my interest in nature photography. Rod is a dedicated naturalist and photographer. Through his workshops I have deepened my appreciation of and respect for the beauty of nature. Two trips into the heart of the Utah desert became true spiritual journeys for me.

In 1998 I attended a retreat led by Rev. Glenn Mitchell. The objective of the retreat was to "use poetry and photography to explore spirituality and nature." At the retreat I was introduced to the idea of using one of my photographs as a focal point for meditation. Later, Glenn showed me some books that contained photographs and poetry or other inspirational messages and he came to my house to see my photographs. A seed had been sown – an idea started to form.

Recently, in the Unitarian Universalist church I attend, Rev. John Morgan started a small covenant group of spiritual leaders called the Shalom Group, which I joined. It is a wonderful support group in which we share our spiritual journeys and try to reach out to others. When I told my friends that I hoped to put together a book of my photographs that would focus on spirituality and the beauty of nature, they encouraged me to pursue my goal. John helped me to work out the necessary details.

With the help of my family and friends, this book has evolved as a natural result of my growth and experience over the past ten years. Through these images paired with simple affirmations I am hoping to share with you the beauty, peace and inspiration I find in nature and encourage you to take the time to be quiet so you can listen to the wonderful spirit within you.

Those who contemplate the beauty of the earth

find reserves of strength that endure as long as life lasts.

———Rachel Carson

I will let go of the burdens I heap upon myself and get back to the basic elements of life.

I will be grateful for the abundance that is mine.

I will contemplate my origins and the origin of the earth.

I will reflect upon the interconnection between the heavens and the earth.

I will start each morning renewed.

I will remember to breathe.

I will let the sun warm my heart.

I will surrender control to a higher spirit.

I will let my life flow.

I will be present in the moment, casting off past disappointments and anxieties about the future.

I will live in harmony with nature.

I will be aware of the color, texture, and beauty around me.

I will find freedom in simplicity.

I will open my mind to learn from all people.

I will look at things from different perspectives.

I will take the time to be reflective and still.

I will try to get to the essence of things.

I will take risks.

I will dare to be different.

I will go where my spirit leads me.

I will look for hidden treasure.

I will dance with delight and let my spirit soar.

I will believe in magic.

I will dream, knowing that dreams can be wonderful and frightening.

I will have courage and be strong.

I will honor my emotions, work through them, and move on.

I will forgive.

I will reach out with compassion.

I will spread joy to those around me.

I will work through difficult times, knowing that better times lie ahead.

I will honor the seasons of life.

I will realize that out of death can come life.

I will retreat to my sacred space when I feel the need.

I will cherish my moments alone.

I will take the time to nurture my body and spirit.

I will share my gifts.

I will be true to myself.

I will live in peace.

I will cling to faith and hope.

I will live with love for myself and others.

*Deep peace of the running wave
   to you.
Deep peace of the flowing air
   to you.
Deep peace of the quiet earth
   to you.
Deep peace of the shining stars
   to you.
Deep peace of the infinite peace
   to you.*

>Adapted from Gaelic Runes
>Taken from *Singing the Living Tradition*,
>Hymnal of the Unitarian Universalist Church

LOCATIONS OF PHOTOGRAPHS

1. Bermuda
2. Eastern Maryland
3. Area of Capitol Reef and Grand Staircase-Escalante, Utah
4. Everglades, Florida
5. Upper Peninsula, Michigan
6. Monhegan Island, Maine
7. Wernersville, Pennsylvania
8. Upper Peninsula, Michigan
9. Upper Peninsula, Michigan
10. Area of Capitol Reef and Grand Staircase-Escalante, Utah
11. Area of Portland, Oregon
12. Upper Peninsula, Michigan
13. Area of Capitol Reef and Grand Staircase-Escalante, Utah
14. Area of Capitol Reef and Grand Staircase-Escalante, Utah
15. Roanoke Island, North Carolina
16. Upper Peninsula, Michigan
17. Belgrade Lakes, Maine
18. Crested Butte, Colorado
19. Long Island, New York
20. Area of Capitol Reef and Grand Staircase-Escalante, Utah
21. Crested Butte, Colorado
22. Canyon de Chelly, Arizona
23. Area of Capitol Reef and Grand Staircase-Escalante, Utah
24. Area of Capitol Reef and Grand Staircase-Escalante, Utah
25. Area of Capitol Reef and Grand Staircase-Escalante, Utah
26. Pacific Coast, California
27. British Virgin Islands
28. Sea Island, Georgia
29. Robesonia, Pennsylvania
30. Area of Capitol Reef and Grand Staircase-Escalante, Utah
31. Robesonia, Pennsylvania
32. Area of Capitol Reef and Grand Staircase-Escalante, Utah
33. Belgrade Lakes, Maine
34. Pemaquid Beach, Maine
35. Belgrade Lakes, Maine
36. Robesonia, Pennsylvania
37. Upper Peninsula, Michigan
38. Area of Capitol Reef and Grand Staircase-Escalante, Utah
39. Pacific Coast, California
40. Adelaide, Australia